Warrior Writers Guide

HOW TO FACILITATE WRITING WORKSHOPS FOR VETERANS

BY LOVELLA CALICA & KEVIN BASL

Warrior Writers Guide:
How to Facilitate Writing Workshops for Veterans

4th Edition (February 2018)
By Lovella Calica and Kevin Basl
Published by Warrior Writers
©2018 Lovella Calica and Kevin Basl. All rights reserved.
ISBN: 978-0-692-06096-4

Book design by Laura Rowley
Pencil-rifle logo by Eli Wright

This book was formerly titled *Warrior Writers DIY Guide: Start Your Own Veteran's Writing Workshop* (2013). This new edition includes significant revisions and additions.

Visit **www.warriorwriters.org** for performance and workshop schedules, photos, veteran writing and artwork, and information on past events.

CONTENTS

AUTHOR'S NOTE: LOVELLA CALICA

It's hard to believe I've been facilitating writing workshops for veterans for over 10 years. We've learned a lot as an organization and community over that time—many successes, many mistakes—and the *Warrior Writers Guide* is about sharing those lessons. We hope this guide provides you a solid foundation from which to start your own veteran's writing workshop.

People often ask how we began. The idea for Warrior Writers came to me after sharing some of my poems with friends, members of Iraq Veterans Against the War, or IVAW (now About Face). I asked if they wrote poetry too. They did—and the quality and power of their work struck me. Others needed to hear it.

I never intended to start an organization. I just wanted to hold a workshop and publish a chapbook. In preparing for that first workshop—which happened in New York City, in 2007—I discovered writer Maxine Hong Kingston. She had been doing amazing work with Vietnam War veterans for decades. Her impressive collection *Veterans of War, Veterans of Peace* (2006) is proof of her dedication. I talked with her, and learned from her. I also talked with Vietnam War veteran-writers

W.D. Ehrhart, Jan Barry, and Lamont Steptoe, to name a few. Their work served not only as inspiration but also as material for workshop writing prompts.

I was nervous before the first workshop, though every veteran there was already a friend. They already trusted and depended on me for support. I didn't know why they felt as comfortable sharing stories with me as they did. They told me about experiences in Iraq, battling depression and suicide, fighting and struggling with addiction. I realize now that they shared these things because we had something in common, something intuited. I also experienced trauma—I'm a survivor of childhood sexual abuse—and I seemed able to provide them with the care and understanding I myself hadn't gotten when I was younger. I was willing and able to listen. I know the effects of trauma: the self-hatred, guilt, depression, anxiety, anger, hyper-vigilance. I know the difference friends and creativity can make. Though I'm not a veteran, I know what it's like to need support in the aftermath of mental and physical pain. And, honestly, I've realized that *not* being a veteran helped during that first workshop (and all subsequent workshops): I didn't have memories of the military, so I could remain focused and steady. I didn't get overly emotional when listening to so many war stories. I could keep the group on track, shift attention back to writing.

Veteran-artists Aaron Hughes (key organizer of the emerging Veteran Art Movement) and Drew Cameron (co-founder of Combat Paper) were essential in helping me organize the early workshops and events. Before the first workshop, I had applied for a grant of a couple thousand dollars and got it. That small grant also covered a second writing workshop, a book-release poetry reading and an art exhibition, in Burlington, Vermont, where Drew's paper mill and art studio were located. The Vermont workshop was an even bigger success. There, the dozen or so participants and I realized we couldn't stop after just two workshops and one book. We had ignited something inside of us. It seemed like everyone wanted to be a part of it. "Warrior Writers" was the title of our chapbook (IVAW member Garett Reppenhagen coined it), and all future workshops would be hosted under that name.

Since the beginning, the group wanted to grow and expand, reach more veterans and host workshops in other cities. We wanted more veterans to become workshop facilitators. So we started writing this guide years ago, revising it continuously (thanks to all who have given feedback and input over the years!).

I've learned so much from veterans over the past decade. Before you dig into this guide, I'd like to share one of those lessons with you. Something Vietnam War veterans in particular have taught me (and something I've been thinking about a lot over the past couple of years) is that the experience of re-connecting with former enemy soldiers and civilians can be a powerful learning and healing experience. Many have gone back to Vietnam, to build homes, to learn the language, to translate poetry, to make friends, even to adopt children. Unfortunately, for veterans of the recent wars in the Middle East, this is still difficult (if not impossible). But there's much we can do here in the United States.

A few years ago, Mural Arts Philadelphia—the largest arts organization in the city—approached Warrior Writers with an idea. We had already collaborated with them on a mural project in West Philadelphia, *Communion Between A Rock and A Hard Place* (2012), and now they were asking for help with a project led by Iraqi-American artist Michael Rakowitz. Iraq War veterans would be brought together with Iraqi refugees in fellowship, story-telling, food and culture. Eventually, these meals and conversations (most of which would be recorded) would culminate in a radio series, with a live performance broadcast from Independence Mall. Of course, we jumped on the opportunity. So on July 31, 2017, *Radio Silence*—complete with Iraqi music, a stage modeled after a ziggurat, and (of course) Iraqi food—was performed before a crowd of several hundred, right next to the Liberty Bell. The show was a wonderful expression of reconciliation and friendship, produced against great odds. Of course, all projects that venture into uncharted territory will have setbacks and missteps (we learned a lot about scheduling conflicts, intercultural sensitivities and rain dates). But many unexpected, beautiful moments will stick out in my mind for the rest of my life. Onstage, veteran Lawrence Davidson and Iraqi

Lovella Calica performing at Nuyorican Poets Cafe, NYC in 2012. Photo by Jonas Lara.

refugee Faroq Al-Obaidi recreated a conversation they had had over dinner. Years before, they had both been at the same bridge at the same time, in Baqubah, though under very different circumstances, each with a very different role: soldier and schoolboy. Veteran Gin McGill-Prather read a heartfelt apology she had written for the refugees and all Iraqis. Beyond sharing poetry and stories, veterans and Iraqis danced together and sang together. The performance, which felt like a new chapter of the Warrior Writers journey, was further proof to me that writing and storytelling really can change lives. It's definitely changed mine.

Lovella Calica is a writer, photographer and multi-media artist. With backgrounds in human development, English and social justice organizing, she offers a unique perspective and develops creative, collaborative ways of organizing and communicating. She has trained staff members of arts organizations and universities around the country on how to better work with and understand veterans. She is part of the caregiver program at the Philadelphia V.A. and is a trained practitioner of TRE (tension and trauma releasing exercises). As founder and director of Warrior Writers, she has edited (or co-edited) four anthologies of veterans' writing and artwork: *Move, Shoot and Communicate, Re-Making Sense, After Action Review* and *Warrior Writers*. She also self-published two chapbooks of poetry, *Makibaka: Beautifully Brave* and *Huwag Matakot: Do Not be Afraid*. She is currently at work on a memoir of poetry and prose.

AUTHOR'S NOTE: KEVIN BASL

My post-Army plan, circa 2008, went like this: I would finish an MFA in fiction, publish a war novel, become a professor and write compelling, prize-winning fiction for the rest of my life. Wishful thinking, to say the least. How many thousands of aspiring writers today cling to such a plan? Well, I'm still working on that novel and the idea of tenure track professorship seems more distant now than ever before (thanks to those veterans and advocates who fought for the G.I. Bill, at least I don't have to worry about student debt).

But I did get the MFA, and I did teach English as an adjunct instructor, for two years. And while sometimes I really enjoyed teaching freshman composition (definitely not the pay), I came to realize the halls of academia just weren't where I belonged. I couldn't silence the imposter's syndrome. The anxiety was too much. I couldn't shake bad days, when a lesson plan tanked or a student got sassy. It was a formative experience, but ultimately I don't think I'm wired for formal teaching.

I do still teach writing, of course—or, rather, I "facilitate," as Warrior Writers calls it. Thankfully, I no longer have to wear business casual khakis or grade papers. Fellow veterans take me as I am. I help them grapple with their experiences and improve their writing, while they help me become a better leader and gain confidence in sharing my stories.

What happens in a Warrior Writers workshop? While the method and tools remain constant (this short guide will walk you through those things) you'll find the meaning, or intention, is different from participant to participant. Our workshops are not critique-based, like an MFA program. Ours are generative and process-focused. We encourage participants to write in whatever way works for them, even to collectively determine the course of future programming.

How do I personally use a Warrior Writers workshop? Let me get something off my chest first. Many Warrior Writers participants, including journalists who have written about us, will tell you that the process is healing. It rarely feels that way for me. Personally, writing is too much work—it's damn frustrating to me—and I've never felt comfortable calling it "therapeutic." I'd rather go for a hike. But I can sit at a table with other veterans who may use the workshop as catharsis, or a personal "working-through" (like journaling), and I can still write and share in a way that feels comfortable and productive. I often leave with a first draft of a poem or a story (facilitators write during workshops too), something that otherwise may have never left the dusty corners of my memory.

A mentor once provided insight on the above concern. Since 2010, Warrior Writers has collaborated with the William Joiner Institute for the Study of War and Social Consequences, a center started by Vietnam War veteran-writers. There, I've had the pleasure of getting to know poet Bruce Weigl. He's included this line in workshop descriptions: "We'll focus on making the writing of [war] traumas a literary and artistic problem rather than an emotional problem." Turning my memories into poetry, often inspired by those things which haunt me most, is ultimately a problem of finding the best words and putting them in the best order (as Coleridge famously said). I may share those words, even see them in print, if I'm so lucky. I feel best when my words rise off the page: clear, concise, appreciated, alive. Is that healing? Perhaps. But it's a lot of other things too.

Warrior Writers means different things to different people and, I think, that's why it's still alive and well, as many other veterans writing workshops have come and gone. Ten years of ongoing programming and a dedicated, nationwide network reinforces that our unique chemistry works. We resist a "specialized" model, and I believe that's an advantage. Some seek friends, while some seek publication. Others just need a place to vent. Either way, we're building community through creativity, and that's enough intention for me. When we get that right (no easy task) other problems don't seem quite so daunting.

I do sometimes think about how best to describe our educational model. It's probably closest to Paulo Friere's "popular education," as detailed in *Pedagogy of the Oppressed* (1968). For Friere, learning is a group activity associated with social action. Popular education is not top-down, where a teacher imparts knowledge before a classroom. Rather, it's horizontal, where the educational content is determined by the local, personal experiences of ordinary people (in our case, veterans of all ranks and service-eras), seated in a circle, face-to-face. Popular education encourages student-participants to be creators of culture, rather than mere consumers.

We also owe a debt of gratitude to an under-appreciated—though once thousands-strong—organization of anti-war veterans. In the late 1960s, the political activist group Vietnam Veterans Against the War (VVAW) started encouraging veterans to speak up, not only in the streets and in public testimonies, but also in popular-education-style meetings. VVAW's "rap sessions" provided a space for veterans to share post-war experiences and stories in an attempt to figure out what afflicted them. For many, that turned out to be "Post Vietnam Syndrome," later called "Post Traumatic Stress Disorder." This was almost a decade before Veteran Affairs and psychology at large recognized it. Instead of silently enduring (how many of us have a family member who never talked about "the war"?), veterans discussed their traumas and shared their nightmares. Additionally, the poetry collection *Winning Hearts and Minds: War Poems by Vietnam Veterans* (1972), first published by VVAW's own 1st Casualty Press (later reissued by McGraw-Hill) has had a big influence on many in the Warrior Writers community, myself included. The book's epigraph is "In war, truth is the first casualty." In the spirit of this touchstone, we ask Warrior Writers participants to tell their stories honestly, unworried about judgment (even if your voice shakes). *Winning Hearts and Minds* includes a section on practical ways to use the book: read it aloud, reproduce it, dramatize it, share it, put the poems to song. Whether consciously or otherwise, we continue on a path opened by VVAW, encouraging veterans to talk about their military experiences, not hold them back.

Warrior Writers facilitators push our model in new and interesting directions. Our workshops can function as a way to process intense, often confusing, events in the immediate. In 2014, facilitator Chantelle Bateman went to Ferguson, MO to help fellow Black Lives Matter activists process their experiences on the ground using writing. Warrior Writers offers a "Working with Veterans 101" class, often presented in business or university settings, that incorporates writing exercises into a program for non-veterans. We attempt to link them directly to the military ("Did your grandfather serve? An uncle? Do you pay your taxes?"). Since 2013, we've gone to Walter Reed to work with active-duty service members, closing our weeklong workshops with a public poetry reading and art exhibition. We've collaborated with theaters, including the Kimmel Center's production of *Holding It Down: Veterans Dreams Project* (in 2016) and Pulitzer-winning playwright Paula Vogel's *Don Juan Comes Home from Iraq*, presented at the Wilma Theater in Philadelphia (in 2014). We test the limits of our workshop model, experiment with it, use it to forge unlikely connections, and we encourage participants to do the same.

No, I haven't gotten that once-coveted professorship. But that's okay. I wouldn't change how things worked out. I facilitate writing workshops for fellow veterans, encouraging them to speak up in a time when silence allows a deadly status quo to persist, endless war is taken for granted, and lies abound. Academic positions are getting cut left and right, and alternative teaching strategies are helping fill the void. I hope this guide encourages more veterans and would-be prize-winning novelists to try a less-traditional, grassroots approach to education and strengthening their communities through writing.

Kevin Basl performing at the Warrior Writers outdoor mural in Philadelphia, 2016. Photo by Lovella Calica.

Kevin Basl is a writer, musician and activist living near Ithaca, NY. He served in the Army as a mobile radar operator from 2003 to 2008, twice deploying to Iraq. He has been a writing facilitator for Warrior Writers since 2013, and co-edited *Warrior Writers: A Collection of Writing and Artwork by Veterans (2014)*. He has also been a papermaking and printmaking facilitator for Combat Paper NJ and Frontline Arts, and co-producer of *Eighty One Echo*, an interview series exploring the emerging Veteran Art Movement (www.veteran-art-movement.net). He is co-editor of *DemilitaRIZE!: Political Graphics from Veteran Movements Against War*, forthcoming from PM Press.

Warrior Writers Guide

INTRODUCTION

The information contained in these pages will provide a new Warrior Writers facilitator with all the information she needs to help build and support a community of veteran-artists. Ideally, this guide is intended for veterans who want to start a writing workshop with other veterans, and perhaps a civilian supporter or two. Establishing trusting relationships is key for fostering mutual support and understanding, for building a strong community. While it is possible for a veteran to start a workshop on her own, having a support network of other veterans and dedicated civilians to rely on will help ensure success and prevent burnout. Such collaborations will also mark an important first step towards encouraging a more open dialogue about war and the military between veterans and civilians.

As you read this guide, ask yourself whether you are ready, emotionally and logistically, to be a facilitator. While working with veterans can be a highly rewarding experience, especially when witnessing a breakthrough both in a participant's craft development and general wellbeing, it can also be exhausting and require more time than often anticipated.

MISSION AND PURPOSE

Mission Statement: Our mission is to create a culture that articulates veterans' experiences, build a collaborative community for artistic expression, and bear witness to war and the full range of military experiences.

Warrior Writers are people committed to strengthening our greater communities by providing creative tools and artistic opportunities for veterans (usually, but not always, through the medium of writing). We encourage participants to use these tools however works best for them. They may want to record personal histories, or publish a poem or essay in an anthology; they may want to speak truth to power (i.e. activism or protest); they may want to connect with other veteran-artists through our national network.

Many find writing cathartic and useful for reintegration into civilian society, and this is something we encourage (though it's not our priority, as is often assumed by those who consider what we do art therapy). *Community-building* should be the facilitator's priority. Our goal is to foster positive relationships both among veterans themselves and between veterans and civilians, ultimately helping workshop participants build confidence in communicating their military experiences. Quality of writing, publishing, and hosting performances are important aspects of Warrior Writers, but should be considered secondary.

Though we are not an art therapy program, the "healing" benefits of art-making, writing in particular, cannot be overlooked. Such benefits are likely the result of several factors: the common understanding and sense of support fostered by a safe and judgment-free workshop environment, a sense of accomplishment discovered through art-making, confidence in performing one's work in front of an audience, decreased sense of isolation (in realizing others have similar thoughts and experiences) and gaining a sense of ownership and control over difficult thoughts and emotions by openly speaking about them.

The above are all qualities encouraged in a healthy, democratic community: all voices are heard, diversity and creativity are celebrated,

A service member reads poetry at a Warrior Writers public performance in Washington D.C.

everyone contributes (and respects the contributions of others) and, in turn, all get to share opportunities. Focusing on these qualities, instead of publishing books, hosting bestselling author talks, etc., will make your workshop sustainable, encourage more veterans to attend, and will still provide a rewarding facilitator experience. Let participants determine how Warrior Writers works best for them. Using "healing language" to describe your workshop may turn away as many veterans as calling it a "master class." Keep it open-ended, and let participants have a say in how the workshop takes shape.

THE FOUNDATION OF OUR CREATIVE COMMUNITY

Our workshops are for all veterans, regardless of service-era, combat experience, or writing ability. You may hear a potential participant say he is interested in attending a workshop, but isn't a good writer or isn't a combat veteran. Emphasize that Warrior Writers is for all veterans and that his writing abilities or military experience should not discourage him from attending. In the context of our organization, writing functions as a means to turning memories and emotions into something tangible and, if the participant is willing, something to share. Writing ability has little bearing on the positive benefits participants will likely get from workshops (don't hesitate to say, though, that workshopping will help improve writing skills, as veterans may come to you for help with writing fundamentals). Again, if the priority of your workshop is community-building (we can't stress this enough), the benefits listed in this section will result secondarily.

Warrior Writers camping retreat, 2014. (L to R) Claude Copeland, Jeremy Berggren, Lovella Calica, Matt Howard and John Fuller. Photo by Kevin Basl.

As facilitator, you agree to respect all participants' opinions and worldviews. This should be made clear in your introductory remarks, before every workshop. Include that participants agree to respect you as facilitator, along with their fellow veterans. Confidentiality is a part of this respect. Facilitators and participants should never talk about what a veteran says or writes about (including emotional responses, like crying) to people outside the workshop. Our spaces are also "pursuit-free." Remind partipants they are there for writing, not for dating. Flirting or other sexual advances can create a toxic workshop environment and cannot be tolerated.

The above paragraph is the agreement that you, as facilitator, and the participants make at the writing table. It should be clearly stated during your introductory remarks (a step-by-step introduction is included under the "Facilitating a Workshop" heading).

Your workshop should be inclusive of all veterans, regardless of political views, sexual orientation, religion or special needs. Inevitably, political sentiments and biases will be revealed through the writings.

NYC workshop, June 2013. Photo by Lovella Calica.

As facilitator, you must remain nonbiased (don't tout your religion or politics) in order to maintain an atmosphere comfortable for everyone. If participants get into a political argument (or similar dispute), politely explain that everyone's experiences are different, that all are valued and respected at the table. If other participants take offense to a comment made by a fellow veteran, point out the offensiveness of the comment and move on. If disrespectful behavior persists, it may be necessary to talk with the other participants to determine a course of action for future workshops. As a last resort, inform the offending participant that he is no longer welcome to attend, until he can be respectful of the others. If you are aware of underlying causes (substance abuse, anger issues, etc.) encourage and support him in seeking mental health resources.

Remember always that your workshop is a safe space for self-expression and reflection. You will be developing a relationship with fellow veterans based on trust, similar to the camaraderie many experience in the military. Participants may talk about personal or painful experiences they may have never talked about before. As stated in the workshop agreement, you must be prepared to respond to them in a manner that makes them feel appreciated and validated, never embarassed or regretful for sharing.

OUTREACH

In many ways, outreach is the most challenging aspect of starting (and maintaining) a Warrior Writers workshop. While there are many veterans across the U.S., they are often not comfortable sharing their experiences, especially with strangers. Participants may attend one or two workshops never to return. This is the nature of working with veterans, many of whom carry trauma from their service. It is important to be persistent, to remove any potential obstacles to participation, and to continue to extend invitations. Sometimes, you (the facilitator) can meet with veterans one-on-one so they become more comfortable with you. Invite a veteran to sit down for coffee or lunch. Talk about things unrelated to the military.

It is likely that some participants in your workshop will be affected by post traumatic stress disorder (PTSD), also referred to as post traumatic stress (PTS). PTS afflicts approximately one out of three veterans following combat service. Other conditions may include military sexual trauma (MST) and traumatic brain injury (TBI). The symptoms associated with PTS (and often MST and TBI) are many and complex: depression, alienation, flashbacks, dissociation and anxiety are just a few. This is a challenge you must be prepared for, both emotionally and in terms of knowing what resources are available to veterans experiencing these symptoms. Do the research beforehand: have a list of local resources ready (e.g. V.A. programs, veterans care centers and crisis hotlines). It would also be a good idea to read the books listed under the PTSD heading of the appendix before facilitating your first workshop.

Veteran-facilitators (or organizers) should take the lead on face-to-face and phone outreach. While civilians are well-suited to help provide logistical support (e.g. administration, acquiring workshop space and getting donations) veterans often respond best to other veterans. An effective approach to outreach is the old-fashioned way: talking face-to-face or calling potential members by phone. While you should send an email announcement about two weeks in advance of workshops, and post the event on your workshop's social media, the follow-up call

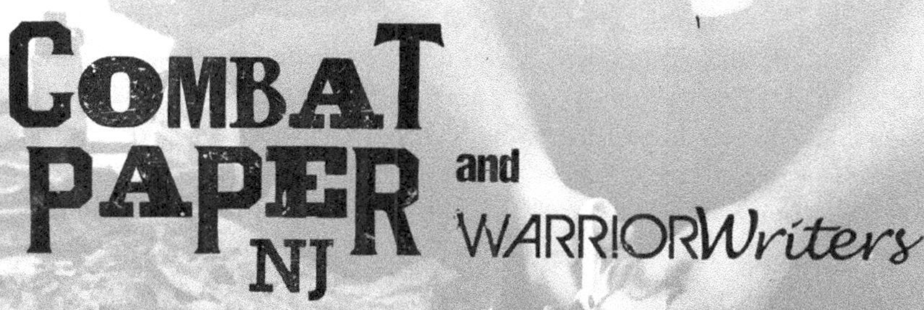

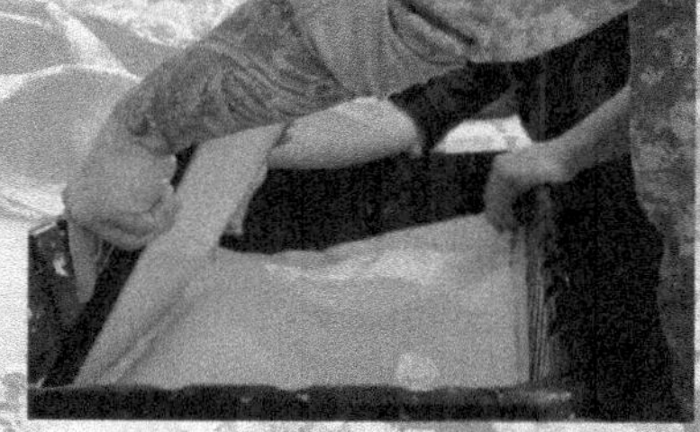

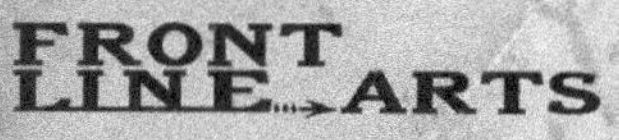

Poster from a USO Workshop in Bethesda, Maryland.

(a day or two before) is probably the single most effective step. Sending a text message the day of the workshop (with all details, address, time, etc.) is also suggested. If you are able to provide transportation support, be sure to include pertinent information in your announcement. Provide detailed directions to the workshop site. Try to line up rides with other participants. You have to make it as easy as possible for participants to get there.

Ask workshop participants to suggest veteran-friends who may be interested in Warrior Writers. On several occasions, we have significantly grown our membership because participants spread the word to their own networks of veterans.

Outreach strategies are limited only by your motivation and creativity. Here are other methods that have worked for us:

1. Flyering can be a great way to find members. Many veterans may not be part of a local organization, but do visit local coffee shops, grocery stores, and universities.

2. Contact (via email and phone) local Iraq & Afghanistan Veterans of America; Team Red, White and Blue; Iraq Veterans Against the War (About Face); The Mission Continues and similar organizations, and let them know about the workshops you're planning. Ask them to send out announcements to their local members and share on Facebook. Try to meet organizational representatives face-to-face. You'll make a closer connection and they'll be more likely to help with outreach.

3. Contact veterans associations at universities (e.g. Student Veterans of America). Ask the veteran coordinator to promote your workshops. Be ready to provide her with flyers and workshop announcements. Request to speak to the veterans association members face-to-face (or facilitate a workshop for them). They may have significant funding for providing logistical and promotional support.

4. Form a group on Meetup.com.

Jennifer Pacanowski tabling at the Dodge Poetry Festival in Newark, NY, 2014.

5. Post on Craigslist.com in the "community" section.

6. Reach-out to Veterans Affairs, Vet Centers and similar veterans care organizations.

7. Start a city-specific Warrior Writers Facebook page for your group.

8. Ask other veteran-focused organizations and events if you can set up a table at their events (e.g. veteran resources fairs).

9. Table at concerts, farmers' markets and outdoor festivals.

Remember, when promoting workshops emphasize *creative community* and avoid political and "healing" language.

THE WORKSHOP SPACE

The building (or, weather permitting, outdoor area) where your workshop is held should be in a central location allowing for as many veterans as possible to attend. Information about public transportation and/or parking should be included with your workshop announcement. It is also important to try to offer childcare, as many veterans cannot attend if it is not available. Make a genuine effort to get volunteers to provide childcare in the same building (but in a seperate room).

As mentioned above, creating a safe space for veteran-participants should be one of the facilitator's top concerns. Accordingly, the room itself should be comfortable. Don't use overly large spaces (e.g. auditoriums or banquet halls) and ensure that it is a private room, with no loud noises, people walking in and out, or similar distractions. You want the space to be as conducive as possible for writing, concentrating and (when it's time) having a conversation. Plan for 5 to 15 attendees. Conference rooms are usually the perfect size for this number.

Workshops should be drug and alcohol free to accommodate for those participants who may be struggling with substance abuse. Veterans with special needs (e.g. requiring wheelchair access or speech aids) should also be considered when planning workshops. If a veteran physically cannot write, efforts should be made to provide him with a note-taker.

Chairs should be arranged around a conference table so that participants can see one another, like a family dinner. Set up 10 to 15 chairs (it's better to overestimate, as you don't want to interrupt the workshop to get more if people arrive late).

Writing tablets and pens should be provided, as well as (donated) refreshments when possible. Always at least have water available. It's also a good idea to place "fidget toys" around the tables (Slinkys and silly putty work particularly well—just ensure the toys don't make noise). Some participants will be anxious, and these objects will help provide a release for nervous energy. You may also want to place slips of paper with relevant quotations around the table. Participants may read them aloud, if so moved, during the workshop.

Here is a list of the best spaces for hosting workshops:

1. Universities: With thousands of veterans using G.I. Bill benefits, many universities already have a veteran population that may help fill your workshop. Contact English, art, psychology, history or other humanities departments about using a classroom or similar space for your workshop. Ask the university's veteran association for suggestions. Be sure to provide participants specific details about location and parking, as campus layouts can be confusing.

2. Art spaces: Galleries, open art collectives, or other arts organizations often welcome Warrior Writers. These are also great spaces for performances.

3. Libraries and bookstores: Check on the availability of study rooms or community meeting spaces.

4. Office buildings: Conference rooms work particularly well and are usually already set up according to the above criteria. Ensure, though, that the environment is inviting and doesn't have a "stuffy" atmosphere. Also, be sure that your participants have clear instructions on how to get to the room, as office buildings are often quite large and sometimes require showing ID.

5. Veterans care organizations are often willing to provide space, and will likely have veterans on site interested in attending the workshop.

Here are some thoughts on places we advise against:

Churches or religious centers may seem like great places to host workshops, though we discourage using them. Related to our effort to keep our workshops politically inclusive, "religious spaces" can potentially discourage members of other religions (or no religion) from attending.

While in the past we have discouraged the use of American Legion halls and VFW's, we do acknowledge that these organizations are beginning to incorporate healthy changes. For example, Denver, CO VFW Post #1 now offers art exhibitions, yoga and—most importantly—has removed its bar. While these establishments are veteran-focused, the prevalence of alcohol is not ideal. These spaces are also (often) politically contentious, with "regulars" who may try to influence the workshop conversation, while not actually participating. While the VFW and The American Legion may be well-intentioned, it is usually best to choose a neutral meeting place.

Think carefully before hosting a workshop in your home. While the workshop atmosphere should be comfortable and relaxed, facilitators should remain professional at all times. Private homes can blur the line between facilitator and friend. Also, because the workshop will be announced on the Internet and elsewhere, your address would be made public. Safety should be foremost when planning.

A note on scheduling workshops: Develop your workshop schedule with your veteran community to ensure access to as many as possible. Once-a-month meetings are a good place to start (choose an evening or weekend, as mornings are usually challenging). A bi-weekly workshop may work, if participants think they can manage it. In inpatient or veterans care center settings (places where veterans have a lot of free time with little to do), a weekly schedule may be okay. Once you've had your first meeting, ask the group what days and times are best. Schedule the next workshop accordingly.

FACILITATING A WORKSHOP

The most important quality a facilitator should foster is emotional intelligence (i.e. social intelligence). By this, we mean being able to show compassion and genuine concern to participants' responses and needs. As facilitator, you will be asking participants to explore potentially painful memories, and, for this reason, you should aim to act as a calming or grounding force. To a great extent, emotional intelligence is about responding to other people's emotions. It's about showing you care. Often, you will be responding to very personal material, and you must do it in an accepting—yet non-clinical—manner. You should be friendly with participants, though you should also maintain a degree of professionalism. Avoid overbearing, "touchy" behavior (hugging a participant while he is re-experiencing trauma, or focusing a lot of emotional attention on any one participant). It goes without saying that you should be welcoming towards all veterans, and should exude an open and understanding attitude. Never make fun of people (yes, it can happen), minimize their experiences or pain, make them feel judged, isolated, or doubted.

Learn from people you know who respond well not only when those around them are upset, but also when joyful. To some, emotional intelligence comes naturally; others have to work at it (sometimes for many years). Remember that a well-functioning workshop requires help from a number of organizers, for ongoing mutual support. Not all can facilitate. Keep in mind, also, that not everyone will make a *good* facilitator (perhaps the moment is just not right).

The content of the written work itself can also pose many challenges. Materials used for prompts in workshops may trigger PTS symptoms, causing participants to react in emotionally unpredictable ways (this should be made clear to the group at the beginning of each workshop). It is important to maintain your calm demeanor at all times. Remember that you have a room of other veterans who may have experienced a similar reaction at some point (perhaps even at that very moment), and they will be there to provide support as well. Give the person space. It's okay to allow a moment of silence. We emphasize that the most important thing is that you, as facilitator, remain calm. Explain that such emotional responses are natural. Talk about how writing and art-making can help us make sense of our experiences, help us process them in a healthly and constructive way. It's also good to have a mental health resources list (holistics too!) available to anyone who may need it. If at any time during the workshop a participant leaves the room, let her go without calling attention to her. Encourage another participant to check on her, preferably a friend or a fellow organizer who is prepared for this role. If the veteran leaves the site with no warning, follow up with a phone call immediately after the workshop. Again, emotional intelligence is essential. With time and practice, you can become a more effective, more compassionate responder to participants' reactions and needs.

Facilitators should choose two or three writing exercises or prompts to use over the (suggested) hour and a half to two hour workshop time-frame. At least one should be military or home-coming focused. Basing prompts on materials from the Warrior Writers anthologies and chapbooks is a good way to help current participants relate to past participants, in turn strengthening the greater Warrior Writers community. It may also inspire participants to submit their writings for publication, which may be used for prompts in future workshops. This helps our community feel a sense of lineage.

Budget allowing, you should give first-time participants a free anthology. Photocopies of poems and writings from other sources work well too. Prompts may come from music, visual arts, and relevant objects. Be sure to change the prompts from meeting to meeting, and always give participants the option to write whatever comes up, even if it is off-topic.

While spontaneity is important, it's a good idea to write down a loose plan, to help you stay focused. You may realize mid-workshop that a prompt you hadn't planned to use perfectly fits the discussion—go with it. Have extra prompts ready for when the group's conversation moves in a new or interesting direction (do encourage this).

Kevin Basl facilitating a workshop in Yellow Springs, OH in 2013.

What follows is a sample workshop curriculum:

1. Give an overview of the Warrior Writers mission, if there are new members. This is when you should remind participants about confidentiality, and that they are in a safe and judgment-free space (i.e., go over the workshop agreement, as discussed earlier). You should pass around a basic contact sheet for participants to fill out, so you can reach everyone.

2. Ask participants to introduce themselves as a veteran and an artist (or art-lover). Ask everyone to limit responses to two minutes. Write down their names for your reference. Introduce yourself first.

3. Read (or ask for a volunteer to read) a piece from a Warrior Writers anthology or other book you've chosen to use as a writing prompt.

4. Talk about the piece of writing. Ask participants what they thought of it, what stuck out, or what memories came up (avoid the question "how did it make you feel?"). Ask them what they liked about it. Reassure them it's okay if they didn't like it.

5. Free-write for five to ten minutes, in reaction to the piece just read. Tell participants not to worry about spelling or grammar—just keep their pens moving. Or, provide a more specific prompt (the "Facilitator's Toolkit" offers many examples). The facilitator should write too.

6. After the allotted time is up (give a one or two minute warning) ask participants about the exercise. For example, was it difficult choosing what to write about? Were they surprised by what came out? If no one responds, simply move on (don't put anyone on the spot with such questions).

7. Encourage them to share their writings with the group. You, as facilitator, should read first, if no one else volunteers. Ask: "does anyone want to share what they wrote? Maybe just some of it? Or maybe just tell us what you wrote about?" Remind them that the workshop is for sharing and listening, not judgment. Don't pressure anyone to share.

In response to participants' writing, offer comments such as: "I liked the part where..." or "[insert specific image] was a really great metaphor" or "the ending was really strong and unexpected." Also, you can ask the group what jumped out at them, or what they liked. Remember that the facilitator's role is not to give critiques (at this point in the writing process anyway), but rather to respond to the content and emotion—the immediate energy—of the writing. Be sure to offer a simple "thank you" for sharing.

8. Provide more readings and writing prompts until time runs out (again, our "Facilitator's Toolkit" is well-stocked).

9. Before participants leave, encourage them to write often (daily), pointing out the benefits of writing and the fact that they will be recording their stories for themselves and posterity. You may want to set

up a blog and Facebook page for your group. Encourage them to post their writings there before the next workshop.

10. Evaluations and feedback are important for improving your facilitation skills and for making the workshop more inviting for participants. After a few workshops, distribute a survey. Consider the feedback carefully and make changes accordingly.

11. Discuss and agree upon a date and time for the next session(s). Ensure them that reminders will go out beforehand. Also, mention any upcoming events of interest in your locale.

You may also offer participants the opportunity to bring writings they've been working on outside of workshops to share with the group. Be careful, though, that any one participant doesn't expect you to use

Fort Belvoir, Virginia. February 2013. Photo by Lovella Calica.

his writings as prompts. Similarly, if a participant talks too much during a workshop, ask him to wait politely until other participants have had an opportunity to respond. Say that you want to ensure that others in the group get a chance to participate. No one participant should dominate.

We've found that a successful workshop can run with a minimum of 4 people (the maximum is around 20. It becomes difficult to make everyone feel comfortable with any more.) 5 to 12 participants is ideal. A goal should be to get every participant to come back to subsequent workshops. Remember that if a new member comes, take the time to get to know her. Introduce her to others. Make her feel welcome so that she will look forward to attending the next workshop.

Toni Topps performing at The Longfellow House, Cambridge, MA in June 2017. Photo by Lovella Calica.

FUNDRAISING AND DONATIONS

Logistical costs should be taken into consideration before establishing a workshop. Thankfully, the basic costs of running a Warrior Writers workshop are quite low: you need notebooks and pens, a room (hopefully provided for free), refreshments (hopefully donated), and reimbursements for parking or transportation, for those in need. Proceeds collected from performances, book sales, t-shirts and donations should be used to offset workshop expenses and, if possible, provide stipends to facilitators. You may also pass a hat or put out a jar at events. Generally, for small amounts, it's fine to hold cash from sales and donations, to use for basic costs. However, if your workshop brings in greater funds, or if you want to apply for grants, you will need a fiscal sponsor and you will need to file taxes (a topic that goes beyond the scope of this guide. Contact info@warriorwriters.org with specific questions).

PERFORMANCES

An important part of community-building is giving the public a chance to hear the writings produced during workshops. Hosting a public reading is an excellent way to give veterans a chance to express themselves on stage, while helping civilians gain an understanding of veteran and military experiences (though performances shouldn't necessarily only feature military-themed writing). If participants have work they wish to share, encourage them to read onstage. It's important to note here, though, that the facilitator should not be pushy about asking participants to read at a performance. Encourage and reassure them, but also help them consider whether or not they want the public to know certain personal details included in their writing. Remind them that pushing ourselves and growing can be uncomfortable, but well worth it. If they do want to share, but feel too anxious performing themselves, you might suggest that other participants read their works for them.

Art galleries, bookstores, universities, theaters and coffee shops are often willing to host performances, sometimes free of cost. Ask the programming director if she is willing to host an event. After your workshop gets established, it is likely that offers to host readings will start coming in, unsolicited.

Invitations sometimes come from the most unlikely places (e.g. in spring 2013, the Philadelphia workshop was asked to read before an opera performance). Keep an open mind and do take advantage of these opportunities. Be careful, however, not to burn yourself out (or the participants) in setting them up. Know when you and the participants have reached the limit. Discuss how often it makes sense to do public readings.

PUBLISHING

Warrior Writers has published four writing anthologies as of February 2018. Our anthologies include poetry, prose, visual art and photography. These collections feature the best work from Warrior Writers workshops around the country. Because they are expensive to produce, we only publish them every two or three years.

Chapbooks (short collections of poetry and other writings) are quick and cheap alternatives to anthologies. Published by small presses, print-on-demand companies, or even DIY at your local copy shop, these shorter collections are another great way to showcase your workshop's writing. Because they can be produced cheaply, selling them may help you raise funds.

Of course, be sure to put ample time into revising and editing the work to be included. You should aim to produce a high quality, professional book. This is a great opportunity to take advantage of time and resources volunteered by professors, editors and designers. However, we must stress: only consider making a book after the workshop is well-established and participants are interested and motivated to do it. Whether or not to make a book should be a group decision.

VETERANS AND COMMUNITY CONFERENCE

Another option for well-established workshops is to host a one or two day conference offering training for facilitators, writing workshops, our Working with Veterans 101 course, art-making, performances and other activities. Connect with other Warrior Writers groups who have hosted our Veterans and Community Conferences in order to get a better understanding of how to put on such an event. They are a great way to strengthen not only your Warrior Writers workshop but also your community at large.

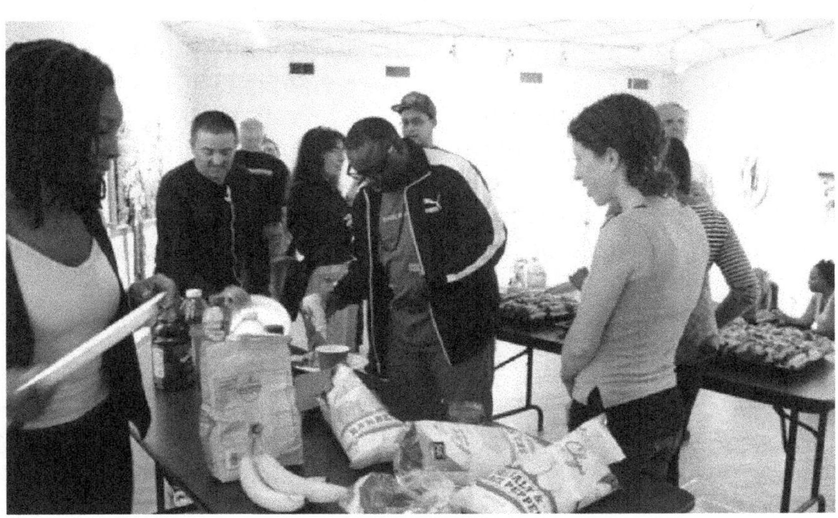

Veterans and Community Conference, Philadelphia, September 2012. Photo by Lovella Calica.

NOTES

Facilitator's Toolkit

NEW FACILITATOR FAQ'S

1. Can only veterans attend workshops?

Generally, yes. You will likely receive requests from non-veterans to observe or participate in workshops, from newspaper reporters to folks who are simply curious. It's best to keep a firm veterans-only policy. Otherwise, your veteran participants may feel less willing to share their thoughts and emotions, thus compromising your workshop's integrity as a safe and productive space.

The one exception is military family members. If the partner of a service member or veteran wishes to attend a workshop, consider making an occasional exception. You should always make sure the group is okay with this arrangement beforehand (but be courteous and don't ask in front of the guest). Also, do ensure that the veteran related to the family member actually wants this arrangement, though it may seem unnecessary. Different perspectives are, of course, valuable. The family member may bring unique creative skills to the group. Also, keep in mind trauma is often carried by military family members in the form of secondary PTS, and it's important to provide creative outlets for these individuals too. In short, your primary participants should be veterans and service members, but it may make sense to occasionally hold an integrated workshop or even, if it feels pertinent and you have the capacity, a military-family-member-only workshop.

2. One of the veteran-participants has stopped responding to my calls and emails. What should I do?

Keep trying. As mentioned earlier, veterans sometimes experience a sense of alienation that may be brought on by a number of stress-related factors. It's also possible that the participant just isn't ready to write and talk about his military experience. Give him time and space, but do continue to make attempts to contact him. Have a list of available mental healthcare resources ready to give him. Offer to talk one-on-one, if you're comfortable doing so.

3. What if I get a poor turnout? Worse, what if no one shows up?

Remember, it's often difficult for veterans to openly talk about military experiences—especially confusing experiences—to anyone, let alone to people they don't know well. Veterans may have second thoughts as the workshop date approaches. This is why it's important to connect with them in the lead-up to a workshop. But even if only a few come at first, keep the workshop going. After you establish a core group (for example, veterans you already know), then focus on reaching out to more people and groups, like a veterans organization at a university.

4. Should I be the facilitator if I'm not a good writer?

The facilitator should identify as a writer, though quality isn't necessarily the most important factor (remember: we're often our own worst critic). In other words, she should take writing seriously and do it regularly, though she doesn't necessarily have to be published or have formal training in writing. As stated earlier in this guide, emotional intelligence is the most important quality. The facilitator should be easy to talk to, approachable, friendly, willing to engage with new folks, good at managing group dynamics, trustworthy, and calm when talking in front of a group or responding to emotional reactions from partipants.

5. One veteran-participant often writes about suicide or hurting herself or others. What should I do?

This is one example why emotional intelligence is so important. You need to be able to make a judgment call: do you believe the participant may hurt herself? Talk to the veteran. Ask her to explain her life situation and what is troubling her. Offer to help her set up an appointment with a therapist. Consider going with her or finding a volunteer to give her a ride or to meet up afterward. Talk to people she knows so they may help too. Remember that while our participants may sometimes find writing workshops to be therapeutic, the facilitator is not a therapist.

6. What should I tell people who want to donate time? How might I make the best use of this resource?

Facilitating a Warrior Writers workshop is different than teaching a creative writing class. As mentioned above, workshop facilitators don't necessarily have to be "good" writers, only competent, calm leaders. Writing instructors and professors, while highly knowledgeable in literature and grammar, may not make the best facilitators.

One way to incorporate such gifts of time is to start a "mentorship program" (this shouldn't be an initial concern of the facilitator, but one that comes after the workshop itself gets established). Professional writing instructors might register to become a mentor, volunteering to work with one or two workshop participants on their own time, to help edit writings for publication or before public readings. Mentors should be carefully considered, though. Don't just accept anyone who claims to have relevant credentials as a mentor. You should make sure the potential mentor at least reviews Warrior Writers' "Working with Veterans 101" tip sheet (page 80). Ideally, they would complete the entire Warrior Writers' "Working with Veterans 101" training course.

If the mentor, or volunteer, is not a writer but wants to help, you can ask her to assist with getting refreshments, materials, and workshop and performance spaces. Volunteers might also help with outreach and fundraising: maintaining a Facebook page, distributing flyers, tabling, grant writing, etc.

7. Should I make grammatical or other craft suggestions?

Only if the participant asks for additional help. If you are comfortable offering suggestions to those who ask, do not hesitate to provide feedback. But this is a great opportunity to utilize volunteers and mentors, so that you as facilitator can manage other priorities. You probably don't have time to offer all participants critiques. It's best for facilitators to focus on organizing and facilitating workshops.

8. How should I handle interview requests and other such offers?

Do what feels comfortable. You're never obligated to give interviews, though they may help promote your workshop. It's important to make the workshop itself your top priority. Don't burn yourself out trying to take advantage of every opportunity for publicity that comes your way. You should also check if others in the group would be interested in talking with journalists. The facilitator doesn't have to always give the interviews—in fact, it shouldn't always be the same person! We are a diverse community and need to showcase that.

9. Should only veterans facilitate workshops?

As an organization that promotes veteran leadership, veteran facilitation is our preference—but, of course, this is not always possible (Warrior Writers' founder is not a veteran!). If veteran-participants don't feel ready to facilitate and prefer that a non-veteran performs the leadership role, at least for a while, that's fine. It is of utmost importance, however, that people feel comfortable with the facilitator. Veterans, however, must be involved in every step of the process, from scheduling, to choosing writing prompts, to determining where performances happen. Veteran participants should be encouraged to become a facilitator, and several people may even share the role, switching leaders from workshop to workshop, or writing prompt to writing prompt.

Remember that it's helpful for a new facilitator to get to know participants before jumping into writing, especially when a workshop is just starting. Schedule a dinner or a fun social activity as a meet-and-greet for participants before your first workshop. Writing and sharing in a group, especially when the subject is war and the military, can be intimidating enough without the potential anxiety of meeting new people.

10. A participant has made sexual advances and/or inappropriate comments to me or other participants. What should I do?

Talk with the participant in a private space, or ask a male ally (if it is a male acting out) to speak with him privately, face-to-face. If you would rather send an email or text, that's fine too. Most importantly, do what feels safe and comfortable. If you wish to be present when your male ally speaks with the participant, that's fine. If not, that's okay too. Ultimately, the offending participant must be reminded that Warrior Writers is "pursuit-free"—a safe space for people to be themselves, fully participating without having to deal with being hit on or spoken to inappropriately. The person should be told to cease this behavior immediately, and not interact in such a way with anyone else. He should be told that if he does not comply, he will be asked not to return to Warrior Writers activities. Such behaviors can fracture a workshop, so they must be taken seriously and dealt with as soon as possible.

Similarly, generation gaps between veteran-participants may bring conflict. For example, older male veterans may challenge young, female veterans, saying they didn't see "real combat," or couldn't have worked as hard as their male colleagues (this can also be communicated through body language: inappropriate looks, for example). Like sexual advances, such behaviors can drive participants away. Again, it comes back to emotional intelligence. If a participant is stifling constructive conversation, targeting other participants directly, or through implication or body language, the offending participant must be talked to, privately. Contests of experience and inappropriate sexual behaviors bring negative dynamics into a workshop, and Warrior Writers strives to challenge such toxic environments.

Chantelle Bateman reads at a Warrior Writers performance. Photo by Lovella Calica.

NOTES

HOW TO USE OUR WRITING PROMPTS

The writing prompts in the following section are best used in a group workshop, though they can also work for participants writing at home on their own. We've included prompts good for beginners, along with exercises for intermediate to advanced writers and workshops. We do encourage facilitators to come up with their own writing prompts, using what's included here for inspiration or as a blueprint. Don't limit yourself. Use artwork, music, and personal objects—not just literature—for writing inspiration.

Following the title of each prompt, the italicized text provides a synopsis and other relevant information for facilitators. The "readings" (or, respectively, "videos" and "art & music") include poems and other materials to be read or experienced as a group, then responded to. "Discussion," which ideally should develop organically based on the questions or texts provided, is to get participants to engage with the readings, to get them to reflect on thoughts and memories sparked by the shared piece. Remember to avoid the question: "how did that make you feel?" It's too general and clinical. Finally, the "instructions" should be provided to participants just before they put pens to paper. At least 10 minutes (more time, schedule permitting) should be provided for writing. Before every prompt, remind participants it's always okay to write entirely off-topic, or to respond to only those parts of the instructions that inspire them. After reconvening, participants may share what they've written and respond to others' work.

All prompts are by Lovella Calica, unless otherwise noted.

Key to Warrior Writers anthology abbreviations:

MSC = *Move, Shoot, Communicate*
RMS = *Re-Making Sense*
AAR = *After Action Review*
WW4 = *Warrior Writers: A Collection of Writing & Artwork by Veterans*

1 TRACING TIME

This prompt encourages writers to explore the past, present and future in one piece of writing. It is a good exercise for people making major life transitions (like leaving the military). It helps to get veteran-writers thinking about their lives before or after the military. It's also easily adaptable for non-veterans.

Readings

1. WW4: "Happy Birthday" by Ben Schrader
2. WW4: "Ten Years Gone" by Toby Hartbarger
3. WW4: "I Have Been" by Rachel McNeill
4. AAR: "A Year of Secrets" by Iris Feliciano

Discussion

Who were you before the military? Who are you now? Did you ever experience your birthday while on deployment? What was the experience like? What anniversaries from your time in the service do you still recognize today?

Instructions

What are some benchmarks from your past that really stand out? What are some future goals? Choose three dates or time periods (be as specific or as general as you prefer: summer 2010, childhood, this morning, 3/20/2003, etc.). Choose one from the past (e.g. before or in the beginning of your military experience), present (give or take 3 months), and the future. Write about these. A variation is to use your birthday as a marker, including at least one from your time in the military. Note what changes in your written response from the beginning to the end (i.e. the tone, subject matter, specifics versus generalities, etc). Do you think the person in your first date or time period could foresee becoming the person of the later date(s)?

DISCOVERING BEAUTY IN UGLINESS

This prompt encourages writers to consider the interesting surroundings and positive, beautiful, spiritual or enlightening moments they had while in the military. Generally, it brings a lighter mood into the workshop (relative to many other prompts here).

Readings

1. WW4: "Guarding Marjah's Strawberry Fields" by Eric Daniels
2. AAR: "Brio" by Maggie Martin
3. WW4: "Sun Set" by Tom Aikens

Discussion

Did the poem remind you of anything? Did the poem make you remember any beautiful imagery, or unique sounds or smells? Did you experience anything profound during deployments or during training? What surprised you, or made you stop and think for a moment?

Instructions

Recall an object or setting you stopped and appreciated while away from home, outside of everyday life (on deployment, at training—or anywhere). Describe this image, setting, tree, sculpture, smell, sound, animal, etc. in detail. Write about what you felt (or what it did for you). How did it affect your mood, your behavior, your day? Did your reaction to it change over time?

THE FIRST TIME I WORE A MILITARY UNIFORM

This prompt is often used at the beginning of Warrior Writers/Combat Paper collaborative workshops, though it can work just as well in other settings. It encourages participants to reflect on the military uniform--what it means to them, how it got issued to them--before cutting into it (the first step towards turning uniforms into handmade paper). It also encourages participants to remember the beginning of their military experience, to reconnect with the emotions, strangeness, complications, and excitement of that time.

1. WW4: "Salt" by Toby Hartbarger
2. WW4: "Medium Regular" photo of Drew Cameron (page 8, before table of contents)
3. WW4: "Grievance Letter to a Discarded Uniform" by Alex Fenno

Discussion

How many years ago was the first time you put on a uniform? Where did you go to basic training? Did your uniform (actually) fit? What are some of the smells you recall from the issuing facility? Did you wear military gear as a kid?

Instructions

Recall the first time you wore, or were issued, your military uniform. Describe the scene in detail using your five senses. Write about your reaction to seeing yourself in uniform. Compare that to what you imagined the experience being like.

Two variations we sometimes use include: 1. Write about the last time you wore your uniform (or, for active duty service members, what you imagine the last time will be like). 2. Write a letter or poem from the perspective of your uniform (personify the uniform).

4 WHEN I SAY I AM…

This prompt is based on "American Soldier," by Michael Anthony (which was inspired by a Carol Wimmer poem). It works well for first time writers, and also for new workshop groups. It is good to use when you want folks to write about life and identity outside of the military. Topics may include (depending on which poem you choose to share): stereotypes and common assumptions, shifting identities, interactions with others (including civilians), heroism, disability, race, sexuality, self-empowerment and speaking for oneself, views on war, etc. This prompt can also easily be adapted for non-veterans.

Readings

1. AAR: "American Soldier" by Michael Anthony
2. WW4: "When I Say I Am Disabled" by Anthony "Tony" Timbers
3. WW4: "When I Say I Am a Soldier" by Jason Gunn

Discussion

What do you like or dislike about the poem(s)? (Remember that it is okay to dislike a piece of writing we share.) What kinds of assumptions have people made about you and/or other veterans or service-members?

Instructions

Structure your writing using the following three phrases: "When I say I am…," "I am not…," and "I am…" Think about assumptions people may make about you. What would you want them to know? What is your truth? Repeat the three phrases throughout your response, if you wish. Also, it may help to follow the same format as the sample poem's author. Consider using more than one identity, e.g. parent, woman, friend, teacher, artist, brother, student, etc. You can also move outside of identity to incorporate actions, e.g. "When I say I teach…, "When I say I believe…," When I say I volunteer…," etc.

THINKING ABOUT VETERANS HEALTHCARE

Veterans often have strong opinions about V.A. healthcare (and the same goes for service members and military healthcare). This prompt provides an opportunity for writing and discussing that very topic. It also makes space for thinking and talking about general healthcare and health institutions, treatment, caregivers and care providers, etc.

Readings

1. WW4: "Lists & Scales" by Chantelle Bateman
2. WW4: "One Year in a VA Waiting Room" by Garett Reppenhagen

Discussion

Have you had experiences similar to the ones covered in "Lists & Scales" and "One Year in a VA Waiting Room"? What has your experience with the V.A. been like? Positive? Negative? How does the title "Lists & Scales" affect your reading of the piece?

Instructions

Write about a specific experience you've had at a V.A. hospital or veteran treatment center. Include some of the dialogue that was used in the situation (by you or others). Perhaps make comparisons to other healthcare experiences you've had. Or write about what the V.A. healthcare experience ought to be like.

TWO PLACES AT ONCE

This prompt addresses an experience veterans sometimes talk about, feeling like one's mind exists in two places (e.g. slipping from a college classroom, to Iraq, and back). This is a useful prompt for getting participants to think about where they feel most grounded and present and what helps keep them there. It can also easily be adapted for non-veterans. It is worth noting as well that in Slaughterhouse-Five Kurt Vonnegut uses the sci-fi literary devices of time travel and alien abduction to communicate this experience. Participants may want to try writing sci-fi for this prompt.

Readings

1. WW4: "When Will I Come Home" by Jen Cole
2. WW4: "Diesel Truck Time Machine" by Nathan Lewis
3. AAR: "Spliced" by Zach Laporte

Discussion

Have any of you had the experience of existing in two places simultaneously? Are they always disruptive, or can they be nostalgic? If it wasn't enjoyable, what will you do to try to prevent it from happening again? How "real" did the experience seem? Did you understand you were still in the present place and moment?

Instructions

Write about a moment when you felt like you were transported back in time. Describe the setting and what you were doing. Describe where you were transported. Was there a "trigger?" How did the experience affect the present situation?

7 YOU THINK THAT'S GROSS? (AKA SHITTY STORIES)

This is a useful prompt for lightening a workshop's mood, incorporating some humor, closing a workshop, following up a "heavy" prompt, etc. It's meant to make people laugh, and in our experience, it's usually a hit. Remember: your prompts shouldn't always focus on negative experiences.

Readings

1. AAR: "Dedication" by Toby Hartbarger
2. AAR: "Itsy Big Ass Spider" by Chantelle Bateman
3. RMS: "Every Soldier's Fear" by Nathan Lewis

Discussion

Let's talk about pranking the commander, realizing there's a camel spider inside your sleeping bag, or the guy who shit his pants on guard duty. Who's got the grossest story? (Usually the conversation goes effortlessly.)

Instructions

What's your grossest or funniest story from the military? Write it down. Be sure to use your five senses, and try incorporating onomatopoeia (the naming of a thing or action by a vocal imitation of the sound associated with it, for example *buzz* or *hiss*). You may want to include how others reacted to the incident.

THE WINTER GARDEN PHOTOGRAPH
BY AMBER HOY

This prompt draws directly from Roland Barthes' Camera Lucida: Reflections on Photography (1980). *Barthes describes the "punctum" in a photograph as "that accident which pricks me (but also bruises me, is poignant to me)." In* Camera Lucida, *he describes an image of his mother as a child in a winter garden. He wrote the book after his mother passed away. Barthes is trying to come to terms with this image of "before-his-time," who his mother was before he was born and after his mother's death. He "shudders over a catastrophe which has already occurred."*

Reading

"Ultimately—or at the limit—in order to see a photograph well, it is best to look away or close your eyes. 'The necessary condition for an image is sight,' Janouch told Kafka; and Kafka smiled and replied: 'We photograph things in order to drive them out of our minds. My stories are a way of shutting my eyes." (From *Camera Lucida*)

Discussion

Camera Lucida is organized around a series of photographs. While these selections represent significant figures in the history of photography, they are not necessarily these photographers' canonical images. The image that preoccupies the majority of the book, the Winter Garden photograph, is not reproduced. Barthes explains why he did not include the image of his mother, "For you [the reader], it would be nothing but an indifferent picture...for you, no wound."

Instructions

What is an image that "wounds" you? I consider this feeling a kind of "good hurt." Before you sit down to write, reflect on the image, study it. Set the image down, turn it away. Describe the photograph the way you would to someone that will never see the photograph. Is there a person in the photograph? Where were you when the photograph was taken? Pinpoint the punctum.

9

REDEMPTION
BY NATHAN LEWIS

Redemption is a common theme, found in ancient stories to modern Holly-wood movies. It's a pillar of many religions and the title of one of Bob Marley's most poignant songs. Things happen in our lives that we are not proud of. It could be something we did or something we failed to do. Redemption is transformative power, whether through action or words.

Reading

From the *Merriam-Webster Dictionary*:

Redeem / verb 1: to recover (property) by discharging an obligation, 2: to ransom, free, or rescue by paying a price, 3: to free from the consequences of sin, 4: to remove obligation of by payment, 5: to make good (a promise) by performing, 6: to atone for, 7: to change for the better.

Discussion

Do we lose part of our humanity in the military or in war? Is it a sin for which we must atone? Have you ever fallen from grace, or fallen for lies...or flat on your face? Have you ever risen from a defeat, or the ashes, or from a stupor? What must you redeem? How do you redeem?

Instructions

Write a story or essay about redemption. If you have redeemed yourself (or helped someone else) you may choose to be a character. You may also choose someone that has redeemed or atoned for their sins or changed for the better. The story may be true or fictional. It may be in the past or in the future.

THE DANGER OF A SINGLE STORY
BY ADAM GRAAF

Military and wartime narratives too often fulfill expectations, and these expectations can affect the type of stories we veterans share. For instance, omitting from our writing the fun we had during our service and the humor we found in it is dangerous because doing so forces us to engage in only the parts we often wish to forget. Sharing more than what might be expected can shift our focus, help us tell our whole story, remind us that we are more than veterans, and give us fresh narratives to tackle.

Video

"The Danger of a Single Story," Chimamanda Ngozi Adichie
    at TEDGlobal 2009 (18:49):

https://www.ted.com/talks/chimamanda_adichie_the_danger_of_a_
single_story#t-586

Discussion

In what ways do we, as veteran-writers, fall victim to the danger of a single story? As veterans, what expectations do we have for our writing? Do you think others have expectations of our writings, and if so, how does our work fit within or work against those expectations? What else do you write about, and why? If someone were to read every piece you've ever written, what sort of picture would that paint of you?

Instructions

Make yourself laugh: free write for five minutes about the funniest story you can think of from your time in the military. Or don't write about anything related to the military: free write for five minutes about your closet or pantry, and then, using the details from that, write six rhyming couplets about one of the seasons.

MY FAVORITE THINGS

Don't limit yourself to literature-based writing prompts only. Mix it up! Music, visual arts and other meaningful objects can encourage participants to write in new and interesting ways.

The first time Warrior Writers used music as a prompt was at Walter Reed Military Medical Center. Working with a group of inpatient service members struggling with addiction, we asked one participant to choose a song for everyone to respond to in writing. Participants weren't allowed to have many personal items in their treatment program. In some cases, they hadn't heard music—something we often take for granted—in days. The writing prompt was a big success, encouraging emotionally-guarded participants to share writing and join the discussion.

Visual art works too. We have hosted workshops in art galleries. We rove around the space, encouraging participants to respond to works that really speak to them (similar to the literary technique known as "ekphrasis"). And don't forget about photography and military memorabilia! Encourage participants to bring these objects to workshops for writing inspiration.

Art & Music

1. Veteran artwork and photography at www.warriorwriters.org (many artist profiles feature artwork, including Martin Cervantez, Chantelle Bateman, Robynn Murray, Eli Wright, Aaron Hughes, Kevin Basl, Jonas Lara, and many more). The Warrior Writers anthologies (except MSC) also contain photos and artwork.

2. Music: Jacob George www.jacobdavidgeorge.org

Discussion

Choose a couple pieces of artwork from the Warrior Writers books. Ask participants for reactions: What does it remind them of? What is the artwork saying? If you're discussing music, ask what people listened to on deployment. What did they play when sad? When happy?

For motivation? If using photos, ask participants to display them. Ask for comments on their own or others'. You can also ask about favorite pieces of military equipment to spark conversation.

Instructions

This prompt has many options. Here are just a few:

1. Play a song and ask participants to free-write in response. Ask: what does the song evoke? What lyrics jumped out? What memories came up?

2. Ask participants to individually choose a piece of visual art from a Warrior Writers book and write about it.

3. Choose a few pieces of artwork on the Warrior Writers website (print them out if computers aren't available). Ask participants to do a stream-of-consciousness, free-writing response to one or several pieces.

4. Host a workshop at an art exhibition (ensure it's a private space. Galleries may let you in during off-hours.) Allow participants enough time to view the exhibition. Then ask them to write about the piece that affected them most.

5. Ask participants to share a photo or two from their time in the military. Ask them to write the story behind the photo.

12 I AM WHO SURVIVED, FORGIVE ME

Survivors of war often carry pain and guilt. We blame ourselves for things we can't control, and we hold regrets, sometimes for the rest of our lives. However, we may forget that even those who didn't participate directly in war are still responsible for it, civilians included (they vote and pay taxes, after all). The burdens of pain and guilt following war should be shared by the whole society. Accordingly, a first step for veterans wishing to move beyond these emotions is to share what they feel guilty about. A next step may be to seek forgiveness: from oneself, from family, from those people affected directly by U.S. wars.

Note that this prompt can raise complex emotions. It's heavy. It should be used cautiously, after participants feel comfortable with the facilitator and other participants. Remind them that while they should always challenge themselves with their writing, this prompt is best eased into: share a little of what you feel shameful or guilty about, see how you feel. Next time, share a little more. Tell participants that while they may feel terrible immediately after writing about such negative thoughts and emotions, they'll feel better in the days to come. Remind them that who we are now is more important than who we used to be.

Readings

1. "Who Survived?" by Lamont Steptoe (*A Long Movie of Shadows*)
2. MSC: "I Am Wounded too" by Jose Vasquez
3. RMS: "I Am Who Survived Forgive Me" by Aaron Hughes
4. RMS: "I Am Who Survived" by Cloy Richards

Discussion

Do you (or your friends or family) carry guilt from war? Do you know someone who has processed his guilt in a healthy way? How? Do you have an example of guilt being used to spark postive change? How might civilians assume more of war's burdens? What are your thoughts on apologies? *Remember: it's okay if a participant isn't ready for this prompt. Don't "fish" for war stories.*

Instructions

Write a poem utilizing the following phrases: "I am," "who survived,"
and "forgive me." The phrases can be used in seperate sentences or
verses (e.g. "*I am* a veteran/the person *who survived* is not the same
person who took the oath/I ask you to *forgive me*..."). Or, the phrases
can be combined and used at some point in the writing (e.g. "I want
to shout: *I am who survived, forgive me.* I am not the person I was. I am
only what I strive to be."). It's, of course, also fine for participants to
free-write to this prompt, ignoring structure, which may slow their
thoughts and words.

13   COMING HOME

Homecoming is a common theme in war literature. Homer's Odyssey *is essentially a homecoming story. "Soldier's Home" by Ernest Hemingway is another classic of the genre. Every veteran, regardless of whether she deployed or not, has a homecoming story.*

Readings

1. "Coming Home" by W.D. Ehrhart, (From *To Those Who Have Gone Home Tired*)
2. RMS: "Coming Home" by Evan Moodie
3. RMS: "Coming Home" by Cloy Richards
4. WW4: "Noise Remains" by Kevin Basl
5. "The Monster I Became" by Robynn Murray (available at Warrior Writers.org)

Discussion

Remember what it was like for you to come home from training or deployment. Was it a happy occasion? Did you feel strange? How was the situation you returned to different? How did it feel to interact with friends and loved ones?

Instructions

Write your homecoming story. Don't think too hard about what form to use. Just free-write it. It can be rewritten into whatever form works best later. Try to incorporate the comments and behaviors of those who greeted you (or, conversely, didn't). What were your responses? Try to make readers feel what you felt.

Beginning writers often hear the instructive mantra "show, don't tell." While there are times when it makes sense to tell (otherwise a story may get bogged down in unnecessary details), this prompt is all about the showing, the sensual description of a place, thing or person using touch, smell, hearing, taste and sight.

Readings

1. MSC: "Dirt" by Garett Reppenhagen
2. "Naming of the Parts" by Henry Reed
   (available at PoemHunter.com)
3. WW4: "Song of Napalm" by Bruce Weigl

Discussion

What are the most effective descriptions in the poems we read? Why are they effective? What are some great descriptions of places or things that you can remember from your own reading (childrens' books, poetry, fantasy novels, the newspaper—anywhere)? Why do you think they remain in your memory?

Instructions

Think of a concrete object, place or person related to your military experience. Describe it using all five senses (avoid overusing sight, the most common descriptor). Advanced writers may try incorporating a process into the description.

 THE LOST ART OF LETTER WRITING

Writing letters is a great way to understand your feelings or develop ideas, especially when there's no pressure to actually mail it. This is an exercise for letting go, for taking risks. Write things you feel you could never say aloud or face-to-face.

Readings

1. WW4: "Letters" by Joe Merritt
2. RMS: "Untitled" by Eric Salazar
3. RMS: "A letter to Myself" by Matt Hrutkay
4. RMS: "Letter to My Future Self" by Aaron Hughes
5. RMS: "Letter to Myself 10 Years From Now" by Cloy Richards

Discussion

Did you write letters home while you were in the military? When is the last time you wrote a letter? Does an email feel different from a letter? If so, why?

Instructions

You can present this prompt in limitless ways, regarding whom (or what) participants should write a letter to. Here are some ideas to get you started:

1. Write a letter from your current-self to the person you will be in ten years.
2. Write a letter to whomever raised you, as though you were still in the military or deployed.
3. Write a letter to a person in Iraq, Afghanistan, Vietnam, Somalia, etc. (i.e. civilians of countries affected by U.S. wars).
4. Write a letter to a child close to you.

WRITING ANGER

How do we represent raw emotions on the page? How might writing be used to work-through and channel anger, a response often associated with veterans experiencing PTS? This prompt can also work with other "strong" emotions: anxiety, depression, frustration, etc. Partipants could be given the option to write about one or several.

Readings

1. AAR: "PTSD" by Chantelle Bateman (also at WarriorWriters.org)
2. WW4: "The Utility of Pain" by Ryan Holleran
3. "Anger" by Mamta Agarwal (available at PoemHunter.com)

Discussion

Anger can sometimes surprise us because it can be so visible—tangible even. Anger is a common thing to face, and we can learn to deal with it in ways that aren't harmful, once we look at it deeply and honestly. Ask: what are some ways you or others deal with anger in healthy ways? How is writing helpful?

Instructions

Think about when you or someone close to you gets angry. What happens? What do you hear, what do you see? What is it comparable to? A storm, boiling water, a car wreck? Write about what it is like when someone you know gets angry, whether they hold it in or show it openly (feel free to use the third person to talk about yourself here—the psychological distance may help). Come up with a simile or metaphor for this anger. Help readers hear, smell, even taste what the experience is like.

17 WRITING YOUR BODY

Your body holds habits and memories. Veterans sometimes talk about being able to feel a slung-rifle, long after a deployment. Trigger fingers twitch when talking about a combat experience. Our voices shake. Our physical beings are connected with our minds in profound ways.

Readings

1. "My Body" by Maggie Martin (WarriorWriters.org)
2. "My Body" by Cherish Hodge (WarriorWriters.org)
3. "Hands" by Robynn Murray (WarriorWriters.org)
4. RMS: "Ghost Limb" by Garett Reppenhagen

Discussion

What memories does your body hold? Where are they located? What did particular parts of your body do in the military? What do they do now? How have your parts transformed?

Instructions

Write about those parts of your body that hold memories. Try to incorporate the sense of touch in describing how your body interacts (and reacts) with the world.

STRANGE GAMES
BY KEVIN BASL

In today's usage, "surreal" has come to mean, simply, weird. But, originally, it was about tapping into the unconscious mind for artistic and political purposes. The surrealists of the 1920s, some of whom were veterans of the First World War, played games in order to unlock those thoughts and memories swimming just beneath the surface of consciousness. One game, Exquisite Corpse, still pops up today in various forms. It's easy: fold a piece of paper several times horizontally, like an accordion. Go around the table assigning a part of speech to each participant in roughly the following order: adjective, noun, verb, adjective, noun (a complete sentence). As the folded paper goes clockwise around the table, turning a new page before it gets passed, each person writes the first word that comes to mind in her assigned part of speech. Fold it over so the next person has a new blank page to write on. Cycle it around five or six times. Participants should not see what others have written until the end, when the completed poem gets read aloud. (The name "Exquisite Corpse" came from a sentence produced with this very game: "The exquisite corpse will drink the young wine.")

Related to surrealism, "defamiliarization" (or "ostranenie"), coined by Russian writer Viktor Shklovsky in 1917, is a device often used by poets. Essentially, it's the presentation of familiar situations or objects, in unfamiliar ways. In other words, making the common strange. What are some everyday objects that veterans might see differently from civilians? How is a piano like a coffin? A rainbow like a picture projected on a theater screen? How can you describe a garbage can or a shovel or a bottle of soda such that readers might experience these objects like a toddler might?

Generally, war is characterized by confusion, violence, cultural ambiguities, and fragmentation. Accordingly, the above two techniques are very useful for writing war poetry. Yusef Komunyakaa has said that his own Vietnam War poetry "was informed by classical surrealism [...] and the surrealist/ dadaist poets." He has also said, "surrealism informed the psychological and emotional underpinnings of [his Vietnam] experience." Many other war poets have also cited surrealism's influence.

Regardless of its origins, this writing prompt is great for writers who feel blocked, or find themselves writing the same things again and again. It also works well to lighten the mood, as the results may be humorous, absurd or oddly beautiful (sometimes all three). Try it out. While the ideas may seem complex, the activities themselves are quite simple.

Readings

1. "We Never Know" by Yusef Kommunyakaa (From *Dien Cai Dau*)
2. "Nocturne with IED" by Hugh Martin (available at IowaReview.org)
3. "At Lowe's Home Improvement Center" by Brian Turner (from *Phantom Noise*)

Discussion

What are some strange or especially beautiful word pairings in the example poems? Why do you think surrealism has been used so often by veteran-artists to communicate the experience of war? Do you dream about your military experience?

Instructions

This writing prompt has two parts, working simultaneously. First, instruct participants to "defamiliarize" a common military object or scenario through writing: a boot, basic training, an aircraft carrier. For example, a submarine might be described as "a mechnical whale prone to projectile fits of rage, usually determined by the grumbling organisms at work inside its guts." For fun, tell participants they may withhold what the object or situation is until others have guessed at it. If they finish before the allotted writing time is up, they might also try writing about a recent dream.

While participants write to the above exercise, pass an Exquisite Corpse around the table, instructing everyone to add a word corresponding to her assigned part of speech. After all have shared their defamiliarization pieces, read aloud the completed poem.

HOMEFRONT
BY NATHAN LEWIS

Often war and military narratives focus on those who go oversees or serve in the military. Veterans are often asked "What was it like over there?" A much less-frequently asked question is "What was it like for your family while you were in the military or on deployment?" Perhaps many of us have never asked our loved ones and friends this question. Certainly they share some of the burden and hardship. Military life and deployments impact families in many ways, often for multiple generations.

Reading

1. "Cool Dad" by Dennis Fritzinger (included in *Veterans of War, Vet erans of Peace* edited by Maxine Hong Kingston. Koa Books, 2006.)

> my dad, who never blows his cool,
> the day i left for Vietnam
> sat down to a stack of homemade buttermilk pancakes
> and poured vinegar on them by mistake.

Discussion

How was your family affected by the military? A deployment? Occu-pation? Who did you leave behind? Who did you think about? Who thought about you? How did your family cope? What changed while you were gone? What stayed the same?

Instructions

Write about your friends and family and how they have been affected by your experiences in the military. Or write about how your commu-nity reacted to you leaving, to join the military or for a deployment.

BEING FOREIGN
BY MAGGIE MARTIN

For me, there were many times in the military where it was clear that I was either an insider or an outsider, depending on my ability to perform. When I deployed, those categories became clear in unexpected ways. This prompt asks you to look at moments of being an insider or outsider, or times you looked at others in those ways.

This prompt can be taken further by asking "What is an Enemy?" Participants might write about the everyday life of a so-called enemy, real or imagined. What does the enemy think and feel and care about? Ask: "What does your enemy think of you?"

Readings

1. WW4: "Nike Boy" by Krista Shultz
2. WW4: "Impenetrable" by Sean Casey
3. AAR: "The Monster I Became" by Robynn Murray
4. RMS: "You Are Not My Enemy" by Drew Cameron

Discussion

Who is inside/outside? Who is foreign/native? Can you relate to the feeling of being in either category? What is actually happening in your body at that moment?

Instructions

Was there a time during your military experience where you felt foreign, alienated, or like you didn't belong? Were there times when someone you thought of as "foreign" defied your expectations or surprised you. Did you connect with them (or make another sort of connection)? Write about it.

THANK YOU FOR YOUR SERVICE

Veterans in the U.S. today are often thanked for their military service. This may come in the form of quiet handshakes, or loud public displays from politicians and sports associations. While thanking someone may seem like a well-intentioned gesture (or at worst, a benign thing, like saying "bless you"), many veterans are conflicted about it. Some feel that civilians thank them so as not to feel guilt over being so disconnected from our military and wars (only 1% of the population currently serves). Some veterans are ashamed of their military service, and thanking them is like salt on a wound. Of course, there are also those who see no harm in it—even some who really like it. If we can agree on one thing, it's that "Thank you for your service" is a controversial topic—an excellent subject for a writing prompt.

Readings

1. "Memorial Day" by Hugh Martin (available at IowaReview.org)
2. AAR: "PTSD (P.lease T.ry S.omething D.ifferent) by Jeremy Stainthorp Berggren
3. "Witness" by Roy Scranton (available in *Nine Lines*, a publication of the NYU Veterans Writing Workshop)

Discussion

Ask participants for their thoughts on the saying "Thank you for your service." Ask: how often do you experience these situations? What questions come up in conversations with civilians? What questions irritate you? What questions do you appreciate? What do you wish civilians would say? Should veterans feel obligated to talk about their service? Why or why not? How can we encourage healthier, more fruitful conversations between veterans and civilians?

Instructions

Write a poem (or essay or story) addressing the topic of "Thank you for your service." Suggest that participants incorporate dialogue, as this subject is ripe with conflict (conflict often drives great dialogue). Remind participants that the conversation can be based on an actual experience, or otherwise. It could be based on something that happened to a veteran-friend, for example. Or a fictionalized conversation that may have happened long ago, or even years into the future. Encourage them to take risks with the writing, to try out potentially uncomfortable responses to the gesture.

22 NATURE WALK
BY KEVIN BASL

This prompt encourages participants to focus on the flora and fauna of a place—perhaps a foreign place where they were deployed. Nature is important for developing the setting, or backdrop, of war stories: the dense jungles of Vietnam, the desert creatures of Iraq, the fire ants of basic training. While nature may harbor hidden dangers, it also presents moments of peace and tranquility amidst violence and confusion. It can help keep boredom at bay. We pause on patrol to ponder an odd smelling flower. We stop to admire a loud bird with beady eyes. Describing encounters with strange, new plants and animals can help us communicate the sense of awe and wonder that comes with traveling to a distant land, if even to fight in war. We should also keep in mind how war destroys nature, displacing and killing animals, polluting water, and contaminating soils for decades to come.

Readings

1. WW4: "Baghdad Zoo" by Brian Turner
2. "Death of a Naturalist" by Seamus Heaney (available at Poetry Foundation.org)
3. "The Beetles of Kandahar" by Perry O'Brien (available in *Nine Lines*, a publication of the NYU Veterans Writing Workshop)
4. "Musings from a 25 Year Old Military Police Sergeant in Iraq; Or... How the Hell Did I End Up Here and When Can I Go Home?" by Kelly Dougherty (available at WarriorWriters.org)

Discussion

In our readings, what descriptions of the natural world really stand out? How is nature used in these writings: is it beautiful, hostile, mysterious, etc.? How are plants and animals used as metaphors in the poems we read? Do you have any favorite nature poems or stories from youth or otherwise?

Instructions

Write a story or poem that focuses on the natural setting of a place. If it's a foreign place—perhaps a place where you deployed—think about how nature affected your experience. Was the natural world a challenge to overcome or a beautiful, grounding force? An alternative is to write about an animal encounter (including bugs and spiders, of course) that you had while serving in the military. Was it a hostile or friendly animal? What did this encounter mean to you? What did it represent beyond merely startling or amusing you?

FURTHER READING

Many of the below selections were written by authors in the Warrior Writers community.

Warrior Writers Anthologies

Move, Shoot and Communicate (2007) edited by Lovella Calica
Re-Making Sense (2008) edited by Lovella Calica
After Action Review (2011) edited by Lovella Calica
Warrior Writers: An Anthology of Veteran Writing and Artwork (2014)
    edited by Lovella Calica and Kevin Basl

Poetry by Veterans

Life after War by Jan Barry
Beautiful Wreckage by W.D. Ehrhart
Clamor by Elyse Fenton (military spouse)
Phantom Noise by Brian Turner
The Stick Soldiers by Hugh Martin
Tipping Point by Fred Marchant
Veterans of War, Veterans of Peace edited by Maxine Hong Kingston
A Long Movie of Shadows by Lamont Steptoe
Dien Cai Dau by Yusef Komunyakaa
Warcries by Nicole Goodwin
Winning Hearts and Minds: War Poems by Vietnam Veterans edited by
    Larry Rottman, Jan Barry and Basil Paquet
Demilitarized Zones: Veterans After Vietnam edited by Jan Barry and
    W.D. Ehrhart

Fiction and Memoir

The Things They Carried by Tim O'Brien
In Our Time by Ernest Hemingway
A Rumor of War by Philip Caputo
Powder: Writing by Women in Ranks, from Vietnam to Iraq edited by Lisa
    Bowden and Shannon Cain
Road from Ar Ramadi by Camilo Mejia
Warrior Princess: A U.S. Navy Seal's Journey to Coming out Transgender
    by Kristen Beck and Anne Speckhard
Fire and Forget: Short Stories from the Long War edited by Roy Scranton
    and Matt Gallagher
The Long Walk by Brian Castner
*Long Way Out: A Young Woman's Journey of Self-Discovery and How
    She Survived the Navy's Modern Cruelty at Sea Scandal*
    by Nicole Waybright
Slaughterhouse-Five by Kurt Vonnegut
Dust to Dust by Benjamin Busch
Love My Rifle More Than You: Young and Female in the U.S. Army by Kayla
    Williams
Redeployment by Phil Klay

Other Relevant Books on War and Homecoming

War and the Soul by Edward Tick
Achilles in Vietnam by Jonathan Shay
Odysseus in America by Jonathan Shay
Moving a Nation to Care by Ilona Meagher
Hell, Healing and Resistance: Veterans Speak by Daniel Hallock

Literary Journals

Consequence Magazine
O-Dark-Thirty
War, Literature & the Arts

Books on Writing

A Poetry Handbook by Mary Oliver
The Poetry Home Repair Manual by Ted Kooser
On Writing Well: An Informal Guide to Writing Nonfiction by William
    Zinsser
Bird by Bird: Some Instructions on Writing and Life by Anne Lamott
On Writing: A Memoir of the Craft by Stephen King
Self-Editing for Fiction Writers: How to Edit Yourself Into Print by Renni
    Browne and Dave King

Other Resources

What is Emotional Intelligence?
    www.psychologytoday.com/basics/emotional-intelligence

Trauma-Informed Approach and Trauma-Specific Interventions
    www.SAMSHA.gov/nctic/trauma-interventions

WARR!OR*Writers*
Tips for Healthy Conversations with Veterans

Veterans sometimes face a variety of challenges including:
- Transitioning to civilian life. Challenges may include finding employment, acquiring VA benefits and healthcare, getting into college, having close relationships, lacking a sense of "home," physical disabilities, isolating, difficulty finding a new sense of purpose and identity.
- Post Traumatic Stress Disorder (PTSD or PTS). Symptoms may include anxiety, avoidance, depression, anger, hyper-vigilance, startle response to loud noises. These may lead to substance abuse, homelessness, domestic violence, suicide. Degree of symptoms varies dramatically. Military Sexual Trauma (MST) and Traumatic Brain Injury (TBI) may also be present, along with moral injury (injury of the conscience).

Avoid:
- Asking if they killed someone or lost anyone
- Asking about their diagnosis
- Asking if they "saw any action"
- Asking if they were raped
- Bringing up or asking about violent experiences
- Pushing questions or conversations (e.g. "Did that *really* happen?")
- "Go fishing" for their stories, pain, etc.
- Trying to get close or touch unless invited (respect personal boundaries)
- Bringing your emotions or traumatic stories to them. If you're feeling emotional about their art or story, imagine how strongly they feel.
- Distancing yourself, as though vets are different from you because of what they've experienced (e.g. saying you "can't imagine what it was like."
- Only talking to veterans about their military service (discuss other topics too)
- Bringing your politics to them strongly
- Compromising your own wellbeing for the health of the veteran (e.g. if you're not a trained mental health professional, do not provide therapy. Maintain healthy boundaries.)
- Drawing comparisons to movies or video games
- Calling them "Iraqi" veterans (the proper terminology is "Iraq veteran" or "Afghanistan veteran")

"Thank you for your service"
Some veterans feel conflicted about their service. Responses to such "thank yous" will be mixed. Many veterans feel civilians don't understand what they are thanking veterans for. Some veterans feel embarrassed and awkward about these situations; however, other veterans may respond positively. Try "welcome home" instead.

Try these positive "thank yous"
- "Thank you for sharing your stories."
- "Thank you for the courage to speak openly."
- "Thank you for sharing your artwork and writing."

Other healthy ways to engage with veterans:
- Your primary role should be to listen.
- Let veterans lead the conversation.
- Remember that veterans' reactions aren't necessarily being directed at you, the listener.
- Respect their space and customs.
- Be conscious of the impression your appearance may give (e.g. body language, wearing camo, military insignia, activist pins or t-shirts).
- Learn more (by appreciating their art, reading about PTSD, following veteran issues, etc.)
- Attend their events. Visit information tables and ask what you can do to get involved.
- Many veterans have a dark sense of humor--it's not always "PC." Keep an open mind.
- Share yourself as a person, as an artist, etc.
- Recognize that they're more than a veteran. Talk about other interests, hobbies, etc.

This information is not meant to discourage interactions with veterans. It's almost always better to make a blunder in conversation than not to talk with veterans at all. Building relationships with veterans takes time. Thankfully, the arts help provide a forum for healthy discussion about war and military service.

For more info: www.warriorwriters.org Lovella Calica, Director, info@warriorwriters.org

Write info@warriorwriters.org to request a PDF of our tip sheet.

NOTES

NOTES